BLADE RUNNING

Contents

Written by Charlotte Guillain

 Collins

Paralympic power!

The Paralympic Games is one of the biggest and most exciting sports competitions in the world. The idea of the games began after World War II, when many men returned from fighting with terrible **injuries**. Sport was seen as a way to help these wounded men recover.

The Paralympic Games take place every four years, after the Olympic Games.

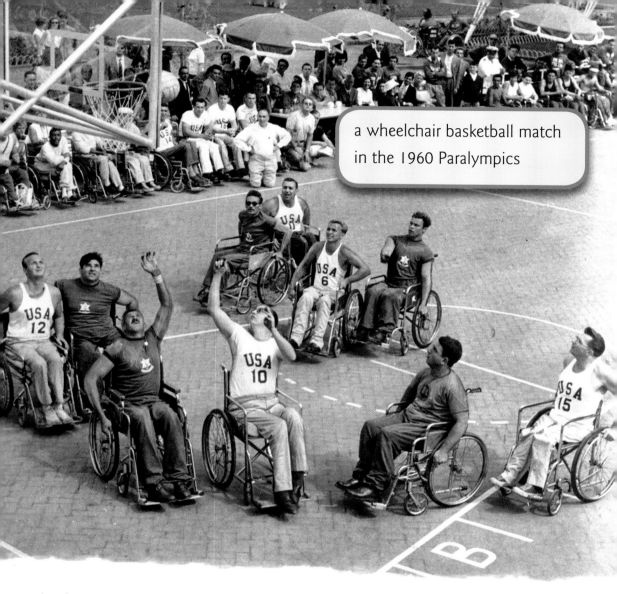

a wheelchair basketball match in the 1960 Paralympics

The first proper Paralympic Games took place in Rome in 1960, with 400 athletes in wheelchairs taking part. Today over 4,000 athletes with a wide range of **disabilities** compete in 20 different sports.

Some Paralympic athletes are **amputees**. This means that all or part of a major joint in their arm or leg is missing. Some athletes are born missing parts of their limbs.

Amputee athletes take part in many sports, such as swimming and wheelchair basketball.

Other Paralympians have lost one or both limbs through illness or accidents. Some amputee athletes are **servicemen** and women who were injured in action.

Prosthetic limbs

Many people with amputated legs use **prosthetic legs** to move around. A prosthetic arm or leg is a device that is designed to replace the missing body part. People have made prosthetic legs for thousands of years.

socket

This is a modern prosthetic leg.

prosthetic foot that looks very similar to a real foot

Prosthetic limbs were made of wood, metal and leather for many years, but today lighter materials are used that bend more easily. Some prosthetic limbs use computer technology to help users move around.

Amputee athletes

To start with, only athletes in wheelchairs competed in the Paralympics. But at the Toronto Paralympics in 1976, athletes with amputated limbs took part for the first time.

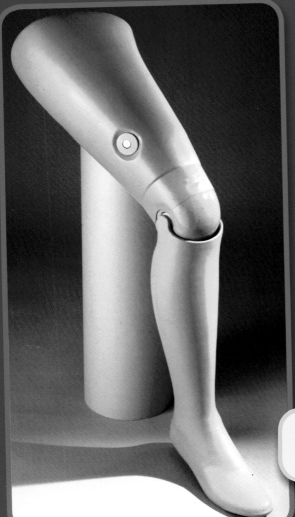

In the 1970s, prosthetic legs were still heavy and uncomfortable, so track athletes could not run very fast and were often injured.

One of the stars of the 1976 Paralympics was the Canadian amputee athlete Arnie Boldt. He won both the high jump and the long jump without using a prosthetic leg.

This prosthetic leg was made in 1979.

Arnie Boldt at
the 1976 Paralympic Games

In the same year as the Toronto Paralympics,
an American student called Van Phillips
was injured in a waterskiing accident.

Waterskiing is an exciting sport,
but it can be dangerous.

His leg had to be amputated but he did not want to stop being active. He decided to study engineering so he could design a prosthetic leg that would allow people to run and jump.

Van Phillips explaining his designs for a new prosthetic leg

Birth of the blade

When Van Phillips left college, he got a job designing prosthetic limbs. He started to work on ideas for a prosthetic limb for athletes. He needed to use a material that would be strong, light and bendy. Van Phillips made several versions and decided to make his leg with layers of a strong material called **carbon fibre**. He had to test many versions of his carbon leg. He was injured several times when the legs broke or fell off.

Van Phillips was inspired by the fastest animal on Earth – the cheetah. He studied how the curved shape of a cheetah's back legs help to move it forwards so quickly. He then designed a running blade that is curved like a cheetah's back leg.

When the curve of the blade hits the ground, it bends down and the runner's energy is stored in the carbon fibre. When the curve of the running blade moves up again, the stored energy pushes up and helps to move the runner forwards. It works a bit like a spring.

By 1996 Van Phillips's running blades were ready to be used.

The blades have a special socket that fits to the athlete's body. A knee joint attaches the socket to the carbon fibre blade.

Spikes on the bottom of the blade help the athlete to grip the track as he or she runs.

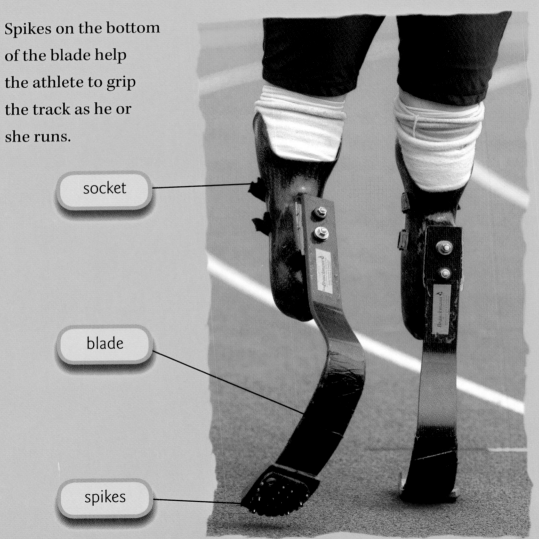

socket

blade

spikes

A technical team supports the athletes who compete wearing running blades. They need to check the sockets fit the athletes comfortably and make sure all the joints are tight and safe.

The technical team make sure the running blades are safe to use.

Today's blade-running stars

British athlete Jonnie Peacock is a rising star in amputee athletics. When he was five he suffered from the disease **meningitis** and his right leg had to be amputated below the knee. He started competing with a running blade in 2009 and won gold in the 100 metres at the London Paralympics in 2012.

18

The British athlete Stefanie Reid uses running blades to **sprint** and compete in the long jump. She is a Paralympic medal winner.

Catching up fast

Today athletes wearing running blades can move as fast as many able-bodied athletes. Some are able to run fast enough to qualify for the Olympic Games as well as the Paralympic Games. In the future world records may be broken by athletes wearing running blades.

Glossary

amputees   people who have had one or more limbs removed

carbon fibre   material that is light, strong and bendy

disabilities   things that limit or change a person's movements or activities

injuries   when someone's body is hurt or damaged

meningitis   a disease that can damage parts of the body or even kill

prosthetic legs   artificial legs that have been built to replace damaged or missing legs

servicemen   members of the armed forces

sprint   run short distances very fast

Index

How the running blade developed

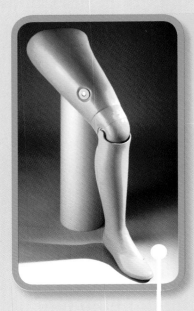

1970s
Prosthetic limbs are heavy and uncomfortable.

1980s–1990s
The idea for a running blade is inspired by a cheetah's curved back legs.

1970

1980

1980s–1990s
Van Phillips develops a running blade made from carbon fibre to replace prosthetic legs.

2012
Jonnie Peacock wins gold at the Paralympics wearing a running blade.

1996
Running blades are ready to be used by 1996.

1996   2000   2010

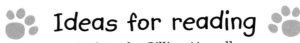

Ideas for reading

Written by Gillian Howell
Primary Literacy Consultant

Learning objectives: *(reading objectives correspond with Gold band; all other objectives correspond with Copper band)* read independently and with increasing fluency longer and less familiar texts; know how to tackle unfamiliar words that are not completely decodable; identify and make notes of the main points of section(s) of text; explain or give reasons for their views or choices

Curriculum links: P.E.

Interest words: paralympic, prosthetic, amputee, competitions, injuries, disabilities, waterskiing, engineering, design, fibre, cheetah, technical

Resources: whiteboard, pens, paper, reference books, the internet

Word count: 717

Getting started

- Read the title and discuss the cover photo with the children. Ask them to suggest reasons for the title and what they think the blade is for.
- Ask the children to suggest what sort of information they will find out by reading this book and note their responses on the whiteboard.
- Read the contents page with the children. Help them decode the words *paralympic* and *prosthetic*. Discuss what they already know about the meaning of these terms.

Reading and responding

- Ask the children to read the book in pairs. As they read, ask them to make notes on the development of the Paralympics, and how the blade played its part in this.
- As the children read, praise them for using different strategies when they meet difficult words, such as breaking them into phonemes or using contextual clues.